THE
COMMON
CORE

Clarifying Expectations
for Teachers & Students

ENGLISH LANGUAGE ARTS

Grades 11 – 12

Created and Presented by
Align, Assess, Achieve

Mc Graw Hill Education

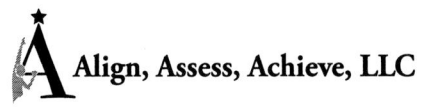
Align, Assess, Achieve, LLC

Align, Assess, Achieve; *The Common Core: Clarifying Expectations for Teachers &*
Students. Grades 11-12

The Common Core State Standards are © Copyright 2010. National Governors Association
Center for Best Practices and Council of Chief State School Officers. All rights reserved.

All other material is © Copyright 2011, Align, Assess, Achieve, LLC. All Rights Reserved.
Cover art © Copyright 2011, Align, Assess, Achieve, LLC. All Rights Reserved.

All rights reserved. Excepting the Common Core State Standards, all material appearing here
is copyrighted and owned by Align, Assess, Achieve, LLC. No part of this publication may be
reproduced or distributed in any form or by any means, or stored in a database or retrieval
system, without the prior written consent of The McGraw-Hill Companies, including, but
not limited to, network storage or transmission, or broadcast for distance learning.

STEM McGraw-Hill is committed to providing instructional materials in Science,
Technology, Engineering, and Mathematics (STEM) that give all students a solid
foundation, one that prepares them for college and careers in the 21st century.

Send all inquiries to:
McGraw-Hill Education
STEM Learning Solutions Center
8787 Orion Place
Columbus, OH 43240

ISBN: 978-007-662963-3
MHID: 0-07-662963-5

Printed in the United States of America.

1 2 3 4 5 6 7 8 9 GLO 16 15 14 13 12 11

Our mission is to provide educational resources
that enable students to become the problem solvers
of the 21st century and inspire them to explore
careers within Science, Technology, Engineering,
and Mathematics (STEM) related fields.

The **McGraw·Hill** Companies

Acknowledgements

This book integrates the Common Core State Standards – a framework for educating students to be competitive at an international level – with well-researched instructional planning strategies for achieving the goals of the CCSS. Our work is rooted in the thinking of brilliant educators, such as Grant Wiggins, Jay McTighe, and Rick Stiggins, and enriched by our work with a great number of inspiring teachers, administrators, and parents. We hope this book provides a meaningful contribution to the ongoing conversation around educating lifelong, passionate learners.

We would like to thank many talented contributors who helped create *The Common Core: Clarifying Expectations for Teachers and Students*. Our authors, Lani Meyers and Mindy Holmes, for their intelligence, persistence, and love of teaching; Graphic Designer Thomas Davis, for his creative talents and good nature through many trials; Editors, Laura Gage and Dr. Teresa Dempsey, for their educational insights and encouragement; Director of book editing and production Josh Steskal, for his feedback, organization, and unwavering patience; Our spouses, Andrew Bainbridge and Tawnya Holman, who believe in our mission and have, through their unconditional support and love, encouraged us to take risks and grow.

Katy Bainbridge
Bob Holman
Co-Founders
Align, Assess, Achieve, LLC

Executive Editors: *Katy Bainbridge and Bob Holman*
Authors: *Mindy Holmes and Lani Meyers*
Contributing Authors: *Teresa Dempsey, Katy Bainbridge and Bob Holman*
Graphic Design & Layout: *Thomas Davis; thomasanceldesign.com*
Director of Book Editing & Production: *Josh Steskal*

Introduction

Purpose

The Common Core State Standards (CCSS) provide educators across the nation with a shared vision for student achievement. They also provide a shared challenge: how to interpret the standards and use them in a meaningful way? Clarifying the Common Core was designed to facilitate the transition to the CCSS at the district, building and classroom level.,

Organization

Clarifying the Common Core presents content from two sources: the CCSS and Align, Assess, Achieve. Content from the CCSS is located in the top section of each page and includes the strand, CCR, and grade level standard. The second section of each page contains content created by Align, Assess, Achieve – Enduring Understandings, Essential Questions, Suggested Learning Targets, and Vocabulary. The black bar at the bottom of the page contains the CCSS standard identifier. A sample page can be found in the next section.

Planning for Instruction and Assessment

This book was created to foster meaningful instruction of the CCSS. This requires planning both quality instruction and assessment. Designing and using quality assessments is key to high-quality instruction (Stiggins et al.). Assessment should accurately measure the intended learning and should inform further instruction. This is only possible when teachers and students have a clear vision of the intended learning. When planning instruction it helps to ask two questions, "Where am I taking my students?" and "How will we get there?" The first question refers to the big picture and is addressed with **Enduring Understandings** and **Essential Questions**. The second question points to the instructional process and is addressed by **Learning Targets**.

Where Am I Taking My Students?

When planning, it is useful to think about the larger, lasting instructional concepts as **Enduring Understandings**. Enduring Understandings are rooted in multiple units of instruction throughout the year and are often utilized K-12. These concepts represent the lasting understandings that transcend your content. Enduring Understandings serve as the ultimate goal of a teacher's instructional planning. Although tempting to share with students initially, we do not recommend telling students the Enduring Understanding in advance. Rather, Enduring Understandings are developed through meaningful engagement with an Essential Question.

Essential Questions work in concert with Enduring Understandings to ignite student curiosity. These questions help students delve deeper and make connections between the concepts and the content they are learning. Essential Questions are designed with the student in mind and do not have an easy answer; rather, they are used to spark inquiry into the deeper meanings (Wiggins and McTighe). Therefore, we advocate frequent use of Essential Questions with students. It is sometimes helpful to think of the Enduring Understanding as the answer to the Essential Question.

How Will We Get There?

If Enduring Understandings and Essential Questions represent the larger, conceptual ideas, then what guides the learning of specific knowledge, reasoning, and skills? These are achieved by using **Learning Targets**. Learning Targets represent a logical, student friendly progression of teaching and learning. Targets are the scaffolding students climb as they progress towards deeper meaning.

There are four types of learning targets, based on what students are asked to do: knowledge, reasoning/understanding, skill, and product (Stiggins et al.). When selecting Learning Targets, teachers need to ask, "What is the goal of instruction?" After answering this question, select the target or targets that align to the instructional goal.

Instructional Goal	Target Type	Key Verbs
Recall basic information and facts	Knowledge (K)	Name, identify, describe
Think and develop an understanding	Reasoning/ Understanding (R)	Explain, compare and contrast, predict
Apply knowledge and reasoning	Skill (S)	Use, solve, calculate
Synthesize to create original work	Product (P)	Create, write, present

Adapted from Stiggins et al. *Classroom Assessment for Student Learning*. (Portland: ETS, 2006). Print.

Keep in mind that the Enduring Understandings, Essential Questions, and Learning Targets in this book are suggestions. Modify and combine the content as necessary to meet your instructional needs. Quality instruction consists of clear expectations, ongoing assessment, and effective feedback. Taken together, these promote meaningful instruction that facilitates student mastery of the Common Core State Standards.

References

Stiggins, Rick, Jan Chappuis, Judy Arter, and Steve Chappuis. *Classroom Assessment for Student Learning*. 2nd. Portland, OR: ETS, 2006.
Wiggins, Grant, and Jay McTighe. *Understanding by Design, Expanded 2nd Edition*. 2nd. Alexandria, VA: ASCD, 2005.

Page Organization

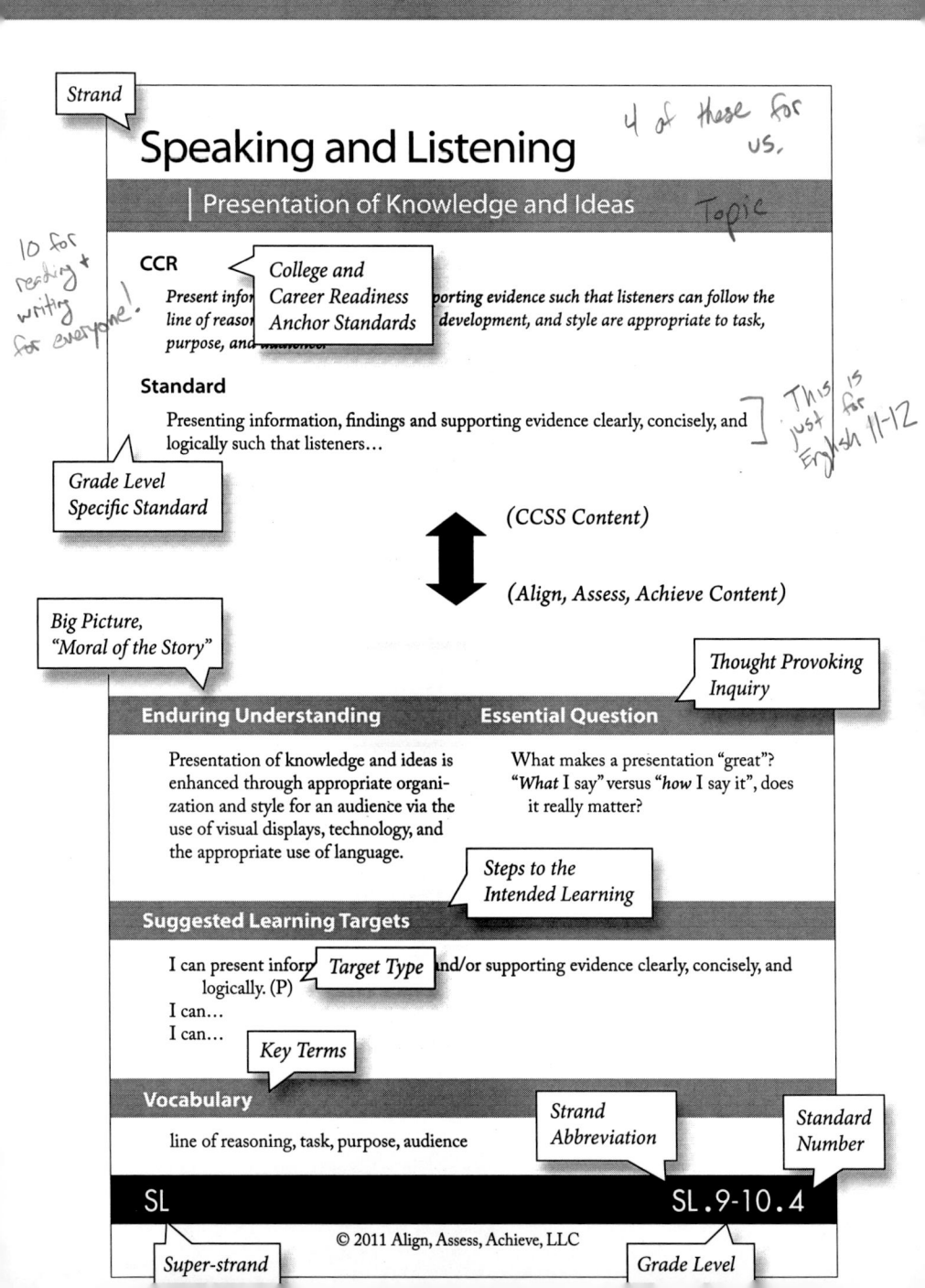

Strand

Speaking and Listening

4 of these for us.

| Presentation of Knowledge and Ideas

Topic

10 for reading + writing for everyone!

CCR

College and Career Readiness Anchor Standards

Present infor... ...orting evidence such that listeners can follow the line of reason... ...development, and style are appropriate to task, purpose, and ~~audience.~~

Standard

Presenting information, findings and supporting evidence clearly, concisely, and logically such that listeners…

This is just for English 11-12

Grade Level Specific Standard

(CCSS Content)

(Align, Assess, Achieve Content)

Big Picture, "Moral of the Story"

Thought Provoking Inquiry

Enduring Understanding	**Essential Question**
Presentation of knowledge and ideas is enhanced through appropriate organization and style for an audience via the use of visual displays, technology, and the appropriate use of language.	What makes a presentation "great"? "*What* I say" versus "*how* I say it", does it really matter?

Steps to the Intended Learning

Suggested Learning Targets

I can present infor... *Target Type* ...nd/or supporting evidence clearly, concisely, and logically. (P)

I can…

I can…

Key Terms

Vocabulary

line of reasoning, task, purpose, audience

Strand Abbreviation

Standard Number

SL

SL.9-10.4

© 2011 Align, Assess, Achieve, LLC

Super-strand

Grade Level

Literature

CCR

Read closely to determine what the text says explicitly and to make logical inferences from it; cite specific textual evidence when writing or speaking to support conclusions drawn from the text.

Standard

Cite strong and thorough textual evidence to support analysis of what the text says explicitly as well as inferences drawn from the text, including determining where the text leaves matters uncertain.

Enduring Understanding

Effective readers use a variety of strategies to make sense of key ideas and details presented in text.

Essential Questions

What do good readers do?
Am I clear about what I just read?
How do I know?

Suggested Learning Targets

I can define textual evidence ("word for word" support). (K)
I can define inference and explain how a reader uses textual evidence to reach a logical conclusion ("based on what I've read, it's most likely true that..."). (R)
I can read closely and find answers explicitly in text (right there answers) and answers that require an inference. (S)
I can analyze an author's words and determine multiple pieces of textual evidence that strongly and thoroughly support both explicit and inferential questions. (R)
I can determine places in the text that leave matters uncertain (e.g., when the reader must draw his/her own conclusions/assumptions). (R)

Vocabulary

textual evidence, analyze, inference, explicit

R   RL.11-12.1

© 2011 Align, Assess, Achieve, LLC

Literature

CCR

Determine central ideas or themes of a text and analyze their development; summarize the key supporting details and ideas.

Standard

Determine two or more themes or central ideas of a text and analyze their development over the course of the text, including how they interact and build on one another to produce a complex account; provide an objective summary of the text.

Enduring Understanding

Effective readers use a variety of strategies to make sense of key ideas and details presented in text.

Essential Questions

What do good readers do?
Am I clear about what I just read?
How do I know?

Suggested Learning Targets

I can define theme (a central idea or lesson the author is revealing – *Honesty is the best policy.*). (K)

I can analyze plot (the events that happen) to determine two or more themes (author's overall messages). (R)

I can determine how multiple themes in a text develop and interact to build on one another and produce a complex account (e.g., *The Old Man and the Sea, Wuthering Heights, Jane Eyre*). (R)

I can define summary (a shortened version of the text that states key points). (K)

I can compose an objective summary stating the key points of the text without adding my own opinions or feelings. (P)

Vocabulary

theme, central idea, complex account, summary, objective

R   RL.11-12.2

© 2011 Align, Assess, Achieve, LLC

Literature

CCR

Analyze how and why individuals, events, and ideas develop and interact over the course of a text.

Standard

Analyze the impact of the author's choices regarding how to develop and relate elements of a story or drama (e.g., where a story is set, how the action is ordered, how the characters are introduced and developed).

Enduring Understanding

Effective readers use a variety of strategies to make sense of key ideas and details presented in text.

Essential Questions

What do good readers do?
Am I clear about what I just read?
How do I know?

Suggested Learning Targets

I can identify elements of a story or drama (e.g., setting, events, characters). (K)
I can analyze how elements of a story or drama are developed and/or interrelated. (R)
I can analyze the impact of an author's choices in presenting elements of a story or drama. (R)

Vocabulary

(No applicable vocabulary)

R   RL.11-12.3

© 2011 Align, Assess, Achieve, LLC

Literature

CCR

Interpret words and phrases as they are used in a text, including determining technical, connotative, and figurative meanings, and analyze how specific word choices shape meaning or tone.

Standard

Determine the meaning of words and phrases as they are used in the text, including figurative and connotative meanings; analyze the impact of specific word choices on meaning and tone, including words with multiple meanings or language that is particularly fresh, engaging, or beautiful. (Include Shakespeare as well as other authors.)

Enduring Understanding

Analyzing texts for structure, purpose, and viewpoint allows an effective reader to gain insight and strengthen understanding.

Essential Questions

Author's choice: Why does it matter? What makes a story a "great" story?

Suggested Learning Targets

I can define and identify various forms of figurative language (e.g., simile, metaphor, hyperbole, personification, alliteration, assonance, onomatopoeia). (K)

I can distinguish between literal language (it means exactly what it says) and figurative language (sometimes what you say is not exactly what you mean). (K)

I can recognize the difference between denotative meanings (all words have a dictionary definition) and connotative meanings (some words carry feeling). (K)

I can analyze how an author's choice of specific words evokes a particular meaning or tone in a text and how using language in a new way creates an engaging overall effect. (R)

I can analyze how specific word choices build on one another to create a cumulative (collective) impact on the overall meaning and tone of a text. (R)

Vocabulary

figurative language, literal language, denotative meaning, connotative meaning

R

RL.11-12.4

© 2011 Align, Assess, Achieve, LLC

Literature

CCR

Analyze the structure of texts, including how specific sentences, paragraphs, and larger portions of the text (e.g., a section, chapter, scene, or stanza) relate to each other and the whole.

Standard

Analyze how an author's choices concerning how to structure specific parts of a text (e.g., the choice of where to begin or end a story, the choice to provide a comedic or tragic resolution) contribute to its overall structure and meaning as well as its aesthetic impact.

Enduring Understanding

Analyzing texts for structure, purpose, and viewpoint allows an effective reader to gain insight and strengthen understanding.

Essential Questions

Author's choice: Why does it matter? What makes a story a "great" story?

Suggested Learning Targets

I can determine how an author chose to structure specific parts of a text. (R)

I can analyze specific parts of text and explain how the individual parts fit into the overall structure (e.g., An author chooses to begin a story with the main character's death and relate the events in an extended flashback.). (R)

I can analyze how an author's choice of structuring specific parts of a text affects the overall meaning (e.g., An author may choose to write in short, choppy sentences to build suspense.). (R)

I can analyze how an author's choice of structuring specific parts of a text creates an aesthetic impact (e.g., An author creates beauty through words, sentence structure, etc. to impact the reader on an emotional level.). (R)

Vocabulary

text structure, aesthetic

R

RL.11-12.5

© 2011 Align, Assess, Achieve, LLC

Literature

CCR

Assess how point of view or purpose shapes the content and style of a text.

Standard

Analyze a case in which grasping a point of view requires distinguishing what is directly stated in a text from what is really meant (e.g., satire, sarcasm, irony, or understatement).

Enduring Understanding

Analyzing texts for structure, purpose, and viewpoint allows an effective reader to gain insight and strengthen understanding.

Essential Questions

Author's choice: Why does it matter? What makes a story a "great" story?

Suggested Learning Targets

I can identify an author's point of view in a text. (K)
I can analyze words stated directly in a text and determine when an author is requiring the reader to make an inference as to what is really meant (e.g., reading between the lines). (R)
I can recognize when authors use literary techniques (e.g., satire, sarcasm, irony, or understatement) to shape the content and style of a text. (R)

Vocabulary

point of view, satire, sarcasm, irony, understatement

R   RL.11-12.6

© 2011 Align, Assess, Achieve, LLC

Literature

CCR

Integrate and evaluate content presented in diverse media and formats, including visually and quantitatively, as well as in words.*

Standard

Analyze multiple interpretations of a story, drama, or poem (e.g., recorded or live production of a play or recorded novel or poetry), evaluating how each version interprets the source text. (Include at least one play by Shakespeare and one play by an American dramatist.)

*Please see "Research to Build Knowledge" in Writing and "Comprehension and Collaboration" in Speaking and Listening for additional standards relevant to gathering, assessing, and applying information from print and digital sources.

Enduring Understanding

To gain keener insight into the integration of knowledge and ideas, effective readers analyze and evaluate content, reasoning, and claims in diverse formats.

Essential Questions

In what ways does creative choice impact an audience?
Whose story is it, and why does it matter?

Suggested Learning Targets

I can identify multiple interpretations of the same source text. (K)
I can analyze how authors interpret a source text (e.g., transform themes, events, topics) in different mediums. (R)
I can evaluate various works that have drawn on or transformed the same source material and explain the varied interpretations of different authors. (R)

Vocabulary

medium

R   RL.11-12.7

© 2011 Align, Assess, Achieve, LLC

Literature

CCR

Delineate and evaluate the argument and specific claims in a text, including the validity of the reasoning as well as the relevance and sufficiency of the evidence.

Standard

(Not applicable to literature)

(No Common Core State Standard #8 for Reading and Literature)

© 2011 Align, Assess, Achieve, LLC

Literature

CCR

Analyze how two or more texts address similar themes or topics in order to build knowledge or to compare the approaches the authors take.

Standard

Demonstrate knowledge of eighteenth-, nineteenth- and early-twentieth-century foundational works of American literature, including how two or more texts from the same period treat similar themes or topics.

Enduring Understanding

To gain keener insight into the integration of knowledge and ideas, effective readers analyze and evaluate content, reasoning, and claims in diverse formats.

Essential Questions

In what ways does creative choice impact an audience?
Whose story is it, and why does it matter?

Suggested Learning Targets

I can identify various foundational works of American literature from different time periods. (K)
I can identify two or more texts from the same time period that contain similar themes or topics. (K)
I can analyze how authors of two or more texts from the same time period treat similar themes or topics. (R)
I can analyze how the point of view of an author impacts his/her approach to a theme or topic found in a particular time period. (R)

Vocabulary

foundational works

R
RL.11-12.9

© 2011 Align, Assess, Achieve, LLC

Literature

CCR

Read and comprehend complex literary and informational texts independently and proficiently.

Standard

By the end of grade 11, read and comprehend literature, including stories, dramas, and poems, in the grades 11–CCR text complexity band proficiently, with scaffolding as needed at the high end of the range.

Enduring Understanding

Effective readers use a variety of strategies to make sense of the ideas and details presented in text.

Essential Questions

What do good readers do?
Am I clear about what I just read?
How do I know?

Suggested Learning Targets

I can recognize when the text I am reading is too easy or too difficult for me. (K)
I can determine reading strategies (e.g., ask questions, make connections, take notes, make inferences, visualize, re-read) that will help me comprehend difficult texts. (S)

Vocabulary

reading strategy, comprehension

R

RL.11.10

© 2011 Align, Assess, Achieve, LLC

Literature

CCR

Read and comprehend complex literary and informational texts independently and proficiently.

Standard

By the end of grade 12, read and comprehend literature, including stories, dramas, and poems, at the high end of the grades 11–CCR text complexity band independently and proficiently.

Enduring Understanding

Effective readers use a variety of strategies to make sense of the ideas and details presented in text.

Essential Questions

What do good readers do?
Am I clear about what I just read?
How do I know?

Suggested Learning Targets

I can recognize when the text I am reading is too easy or too difficult for me. (K)
I can determine reading strategies (e.g., ask questions, make connections, take notes, make inferences, visualize, re-read) that will help me comprehend difficult texts. (S)

Vocabulary

reading strategy, comprehension

R   RL.12.10

© 2011 Align, Assess, Achieve, LLC

Informational Text

CCR

Read closely to determine what the text says explicitly and to make logical inferences from it; cite specific textual evidence when writing or speaking to support conclusions drawn from the text.

Standard

Cite strong and thorough textual evidence to support analysis of what the text says explicitly as well as inferences drawn from the text, including determining where the text leaves matters uncertain.

Enduring Understanding

Effective readers use a variety of strategies to make sense of key ideas and details presented in text.

Essential Questions

What do good readers do?
Am I clear about what I just read?
How do I know?

Suggested Learning Targets

I can define textual evidence ("word for word" support). (K)
I can define inference and explain how a reader uses textual evidence to reach a logical conclusion ("based on what I've read, it's most likely true that…"). (R)
I can read closely and find answers explicitly in text (right there answers) and answers that require an inference. (S)
I can analyze an author's words and determine multiple pieces of textual evidence that strongly and thoroughly support both explicit and inferential questions. (R)
I can determine places in the text that leave matters uncertain (e.g., when the reader must draw his/her own conclusions/assumptions). (R)

Vocabulary

textual evidence, analyze, inference, explicit

R   RI.11-12.1

© 2011 Align, Assess, Achieve, LLC

Informational Text

CCR

Determine central ideas or themes of a text and analyze their development; summarize the key supporting details and ideas.

Standard

Determine two or more central ideas of a text and analyze their development over the course of the text, including how they interact and build on one another to provide a complex analysis; provide an objective summary of the text.

Enduring Understanding

Effective readers use a variety of strategies to make sense of key ideas and details presented in text.

Essential Questions

What do good readers do?
Am I clear about what I just read?
How do I know?

Suggested Learning Targets

I can define central idea (main point in a piece of writing). (K)
I can determine two or more central ideas of a text. (R)
I can determine how two or more central ideas of a text interact and build on one another to develop a text with complex meaning. (R)
I can analyze how central ideas develop over the course of a text. (R)
I can compose an objective summary stating the key points of the text without adding my own opinions or feelings. (P)

Vocabulary

central idea

R

RI.11-12.2

© 2011 Align, Assess, Achieve, LLC

Informational Text

CCR

Analyze how and why individuals, events, and ideas develop and interact over the course of a text.

Standard

Analyze a complex set of ideas or sequence of events and explain how specific individuals, ideas, or events interact and develop over the course of the text.

Enduring Understanding

Effective readers use a variety of strategies to make sense of key ideas and details presented in text.

Essential Questions

What do good readers do?
Am I clear about what I just read?
How do I know?

Suggested Learning Targets

I can determine a complex set of ideas or sequence of events conveyed in a text. (R)
I can analyze how specific individuals interact and develop within a complex set of ideas or sequence of events. (R)
I can analyze how specific ideas interact and develop within a complex set of ideas or sequence of events. (R)
I can analyze how specific events interact and develop within a complex set of ideas or sequence of events. (R)

(No applicable vocabulary)

R   RI.11-12.3

© 2011 Align, Assess, Achieve, LLC

Informational Text

CCR

Interpret words and phrases as they are used in a text, including determining technical, connotative, and figurative meanings, and analyze how specific word choices shape meaning or tone.

Standard

Determine the meaning of words and phrases as they are used in a text, including figurative, connotative, and technical meanings; analyze how an author uses and refines the meaning of a key term or terms over the course of a text (e.g., how Madison defines *faction* in *Federalist* No. 10).

Enduring Understanding

Analyzing texts for structure, purpose, and viewpoint allows an effective reader to gain insight and strengthen understanding.

Essential Questions

Author's choice: Why does it matter? What makes a story a "great" story?

Suggested Learning Targets

I can define and identify various forms of figurative language (e.g., simile, metaphor, hyperbole, personification, alliteration, onomatopoeia). (K)

I can distinguish between literal language (it means exactly what it says) and figurative language (sometimes what you say is not exactly what you mean). (K)

I can recognize the difference between denotative meanings (all words have a dictionary definition) and connotative meanings (some words carry feeling). (K)

I can recognize words that have technical meaning and understand their purpose in a specific text (e.g., "stem" in an article about flowers versus "stem" in an article about cell research). (R)

I can analyze how a key term or terms are used and refined over the course of a text. (R)

Vocabulary

figurative language, literal language, denotative meaning, connotative meaning, technical meaning, refine

R

RI.11-12.4

© 2011 Align, Assess, Achieve, LLC

Informational Text

CCR

Analyze the structure of texts, including how specific sentences, paragraphs, and larger portions of the text (e.g., a section, chapter, scene, or stanza) relate to each other and the whole.

Standard

Analyze and evaluate the effectiveness of the structure an author uses in his or her exposition or argument, including whether the structure makes points clear, convincing, and engaging.

Enduring Understanding

Analyzing texts for structure, purpose, and viewpoint allows an effective reader to gain insight and strengthen understanding.

Essential Questions

Author's choice: Why does it matter? What makes a story a "great" story?

Suggested Learning Targets

I can determine how an author chose to structure his/her exposition or argument (e.g., chronological, cause and effect, problem and solution, compare and contrast). (R)

I can analyze the structure of an author's exposition or argument and evaluate whether the structure is effective. (R)

I can determine if an author's structure is effective in making his/her points clear, convincing, and engaging. (R)

I can evaluate how an author's choice of structure impacts his/her audience. (R)

Vocabulary

exposition

R

RI.11-12.5

© 2011 Align, Assess, Achieve, LLC

Informational Text

CCR

Assess how point of view or purpose shapes the content and style of a text.

Standard

Determine an author's point of view or purpose in a text in which the rhetoric is particularly effective, analyzing how style and content contribute to the power, persuasiveness or beauty of the text.

Enduring Understanding

Analyzing texts for structure, purpose, and viewpoint allows an effective reader to gain insight and strengthen understanding.

Essential Questions

Author's choice: Why does it matter? What makes a story a "great" story?

Suggested Learning Targets

I can define point of view as how the author feels about the situation/topic of a text. (K)

I can determine an author's point of view (*What do I know about the author's opinions, values, and/or beliefs?*) and explain his/her purpose for writing the text. (R)

I can define rhetoric (a technique an author uses to persuade a reader to consider a topic from a different perspective). (K)

I can identify when an author uses rhetoric and analyze how the rhetoric strengthens his/her point of view or purpose. (R)

I can analyze how the author's style and content contribute to the power, persuasiveness, or beauty of the text. (R)

Vocabulary

point of view, purpose, rhetoric

R

RI.11-12.6

© 2011 Align, Assess, Achieve, LLC

Informational Text

CCR

*Integrate and evaluate content presented in diverse media and formats, including visually and quantitatively, as well as in words.**

Standard

Integrate and evaluate multiple sources of information presented in different media or formats (e.g., visually, quantitatively) as well as in words in order to address a question or solve a problem.

Please see "Research to Build Knowledge" in Writing and "Comprehension and Collaboration" in Speaking and Listening for additional standards relevant to gathering, assessing, and applying information from print and digital sources.

Enduring Understanding

To gain keener insight into the integration of knowledge and ideas, effective readers analyze and evaluate content, reasoning, and claims in diverse formats.

Essential Questions

In what ways does creative choice impact an audience?
Whose story is it, and why does it matter?

Suggested Learning Targets

I can identify multiple sources of information presented in different media or formats as well as in words to assist me in addressing a question or solving a problem. (K)
I can evaluate information I have gathered and determine its effectiveness in assisting me to address a question or solve a problem. (R)
I can integrate effective information I have gathered to answer a question or solve a problem. (S)

Vocabulary

integrate

R

RI.11-12.7

© 2011 Align, Assess, Achieve, LLC

Informational Text

CCR

Delineate and evaluate the argument and specific claims in a text, including the validity of the reasoning as well as the relevance and sufficiency of the evidence.

Standard

Delineate and evaluate the reasoning in seminal U.S. texts, including the application of constitutional principles and use of legal reasoning (e.g., in U.S. Supreme Court majority opinions and dissents) and the premises, purposes, and arguments in works of public advocacy (e.g., *The Federalist*, presidential addresses).

Enduring Understanding

To gain keener insight into the integration of knowledge and ideas, effective readers analyze and evaluate content, reasoning, and claims in diverse formats.

Essential Questions

In what ways does creative choice impact an audience?
Whose story is it, and why does it matter?

Suggested Learning Targets

I can determine the purpose behind the creation of seminal U.S. texts. (R)
I can identify constitutional principles and /or legal reasoning found in seminal U.S. texts. (K)
I can delineate (outline) and evaluate the application of constitutional principles and the use of legal reasoning in seminal U.S. texts. (P)
I can identify the premises, purposes, and arguments found in works of public advocacy. (K)
I can delineate (outline) and evaluate the premises, purposes, and arguments found in works of public advocacy. (P)

Vocabulary

seminal U.S. text, constitutional principle, work of public advocacy

R

RI.11-12.8

© 2011 Align, Assess, Achieve, LLC

Informational Text

CCR

Analyze how two or more texts address similar themes or topics in order to build knowledge or to compare the approaches the authors take.

Standard

Analyze seventeenth-, eighteenth-, and nineteenth-century foundational U.S. documents of historical and literary significance (including The Declaration of Independence, the Preamble to the Constitution, the Bill of Rights, and Lincoln's Second Inaugural Address) for their themes, purposes, and rhetorical features.

Enduring Understanding

To gain keener insight into the integration of knowledge and ideas, effective readers analyze and evaluate content, reasoning, and claims in diverse formats.

Essential Questions

In what ways does creative choice impact an audience?
Whose story is it, and why does it matter?

Suggested Learning Targets

I can identify various foundational U.S. documents of historical and literary significance from different time periods. (K)
I can identify themes, purposes, and rhetorical features used in various foundational U.S. documents of historical and literary significance. (K)
I can analyze how different foundational U.S. documents utilize themes (e.g., freedom, independence, equality). (R)
I can analyze how different foundational U.S. documents utilize rhetorical features (e.g., allusion, anecdote, appeal to authority). (R)

Vocabulary

foundational U.S. document, rhetorical feature

R

RI.11-12.9

© 2011 Align, Assess, Achieve, LLC

Informational Text

CCR

Read and comprehend complex literary and informational texts independently and proficiently.

Standard

By the end of grade 11, read and comprehend literary nonfiction in the grades 11–CCR text complexity band proficiently, with scaffolding as needed at the high end of the range.

Enduring Understanding

Effective readers use a variety of strategies to make sense of the ideas and details presented in text.

Essential Questions

What do good readers do?
Am I clear about what I just read?
How do I know?

Suggested Learning Targets

I can recognize when the text I am reading is too easy or too difficult for me. (K)
I can determine reading strategies (e.g., ask questions, make connections, take notes, make inferences, visualize, re-read) that will help me comprehend difficult texts. (S)

Vocabulary

(No applicable vocabulary)

R   RI.11.10

© 2011 Align, Assess, Achieve, LLC

Informational Text

CCR

Read and comprehend complex literary and informational texts independently and proficiently.

Standard

By the end of grade 12, read and comprehend literary nonfiction at the high end of the grades 11–CCR text complexity band independently and proficiently.

Enduring Understanding

Effective readers use a variety of strategies to make sense of the ideas and details presented in text.

Essential Questions

What do good readers do?
Am I clear about what I just read?
How do I know?

Suggested Learning Targets

I can recognize when the text I am reading is too easy or too difficult for me. (K)
I can determine reading strategies (e.g., ask questions, make connections, take notes, make inferences, visualize, re-read) that will help me comprehend difficult texts. (S)

Vocabulary

(No applicable vocabulary)

R

RI.12.10

© 2011 Align, Assess, Achieve, LLC

Writing

CCR

Write arguments to support claims in an analysis of substantive topics or texts, using valid reasoning and relevant and sufficient evidence.

Standard

Write arguments to support claims in an analysis of substantive topics or texts, using valid reasoning and relevant and sufficient evidence.

a. Introduce precise, knowledgeable claim(s), establish the significance of the claim(s), distinguish the claim(s) from alternate or opposing claims, and create an organization that logically sequences claim(s), counterclaims, reasons, and evidence.

b. Develop claim(s) and counterclaims fairly and thoroughly, supplying the most relevant evidence for each while pointing out the strengths and limitations of both in a manner that anticipates the audience's knowledge level, concerns, values, and possible biases.

c. Use words, phrases, and clauses as well as varied syntax to link the major sections of the text, create cohesion, and clarify the relationships between claim(s) and reasons, between reasons and evidence, and between claim(s) and counterclaims.

d. Establish and maintain a formal style and objective tone while attending to the norms and conventions of the discipline in which they are writing.

e. Provide a concluding statement or section that follows from and supports the argument presented.

*These broad types of writing include many subgenres. See Appendix A for definitions of key writing types.

Enduring Understanding

Writing should be purposely focused, detailed, organized, and sequenced in a way that clearly communicates the ideas to the reader.

Essential Questions

What do good writers do?
What's my purpose and how do I develop it?

Suggested Learning Targets

I can analyze substantive (influential) topics or texts to determine an argument that causes or has caused a debate in society. (R)

(continued on next page)

Vocabulary

claim, counterclaim, syntax

W   **W.11-12.1**

© 2011 Align, Assess, Achieve, LLC

Writing

CCR

Write arguments to support claims in an analysis of substantive topics or texts, using valid reasoning and relevant and sufficient evidence.

Standard

Write arguments to support claims in an analysis of substantive topics or texts, using valid reasoning and relevant and sufficient evidence.

a. Introduce precise, knowledgeable claim(s), establish the significance of the claim(s), distinguish the claim(s) from alternate or opposing claims, and create an organization that logically sequences claim(s), counterclaims, reasons, and evidence.

b. Develop claim(s) and counterclaims fairly and thoroughly, supplying the most relevant evidence for each while pointing out the strengths and limitations of both in a manner that anticipates the audience's knowledge level, concerns, values, and possible biases.

c. Use words, phrases, and clauses as well as varied syntax to link the major sections of the text, create cohesion, and clarify the relationships between claim(s) and reasons, between reasons and evidence, and between claim(s) and counterclaims.

d. Establish and maintain a formal style and objective tone while attending to the norms and conventions of the discipline in which they are writing.

e. Provide a concluding statement or section that follows from and supports the argument presented.

*These broad types of writing include many subgenres. See Appendix A for definitions of key writing types.

Suggested Learning Targets

(continued from previous page)

I can choose a side of the argument, identify precise, knowledgeable claims, and establish the significance of the claim(s). (S)

I can identify alternate or opposing claims that counter my argument. (K)

I can organize claims, counterclaims, reasons, and evidence into a logical sequence. (S)

I can anticipate my audience's knowledge level, concerns, values, and possible biases and develop my claims and counterclaims by pointing out the most relevant strengths and limitations of both. (S)

I can present my argument in a formal style and objective tone. (P)

I can create cohesion and clarify relationships among claims and counterclaims using transitions as well as varied syntax. (P)

I can provide a concluding statement/section that supports my argument. (P)

© 2011 Align, Assess, Achieve, LLC

Writing

CCR

Write informative/explanatory texts to examine and convey complex ideas and information clearly and accurately through the effective selection, organization, and analysis of content.

Standard

Write informative/explanatory texts to examine and convey complex ideas, concepts, and information clearly and accurately through the effective selection, organization, and analysis of content.

a. Introduce a topic; organize complex ideas, concepts, and information so that each new element builds on that which precedes it to create a unified whole; include formatting (e.g., headings), graphics (e.g., figures, tables), and multimedia when useful to aiding comprehension.

b. Develop the topic thoroughly by selecting the most significant and relevant facts, extended definitions, concrete details, quotations, or other information and examples appropriate to the audience's knowledge of the topic.

c. Use appropriate and varied transitions and syntax to link the major sections of the text, create cohesion, and clarify the relationships among complex ideas and concepts.

d. Use precise language, domain-specific vocabulary, and techniques such as metaphor, simile, and analogy to manage the complexity of the topic.

e. Establish and maintain a formal style and objective tone while attending to the norms and conventions of the discipline in which they are writing.

f. Provide a concluding statement or section that follows from and supports the information or explanation presented (e.g., articulating implications or the significance of the topic).

*These types of writing include many subgenres. See Appendix A for definitions of key writing types.

Enduring Understanding

Writing should be purposely focused, detailed, organized, and sequenced in a way that clearly communicates the ideas to the reader.

Essential Questions

What do good writers do?
What's my purpose and how do I develop it?

Suggested Learning Targets

I can choose a topic and identify and select the most significant and relevant information (e.g., well-chosen facts, extended definitions, concrete details, quotations, examples) to develop and share with my audience. (S)

(continued on next page)

Vocabulary

organizational structure, formatting structure, domain-specific vocabulary, syntax

W   W.11-12.2

© 2011 Align, Assess, Achieve, LLC

Writing

CCR

Write informative/explanatory texts to examine and convey complex ideas and information clearly and accurately through the effective selection, organization, and analysis of content.

Standard

Write informative/explanatory texts to examine and convey complex ideas, concepts, and information clearly and accurately through the effective selection, organization, and analysis of content.

a. Introduce a topic; organize complex ideas, concepts, and information so that each new element builds on that which precedes it to create a unified whole; include formatting (e.g., headings), graphics (e.g., figures, tables), and multimedia when useful to aiding comprehension.

b. Develop the topic thoroughly by selecting the most significant and relevant facts, extended definitions, concrete details, quotations, or other information and examples appropriate to the audience's knowledge of the topic.

c. Use appropriate and varied transitions and syntax to link the major sections of the text, create cohesion, and clarify the relationships among complex ideas and concepts.

d. Use precise language, domain-specific vocabulary, and techniques such as metaphor, simile, and analogy to manage the complexity of the topic.

e. Establish and maintain a formal style and objective tone while attending to the norms and conventions of the discipline in which they are writing.

f. Provide a concluding statement or section that follows from and supports the information or explanation presented (e.g., articulating implications or the significance of the topic).

These broad types of writing include many subgenres. See Appendix A for definitions of key writing types.

Suggested Learning Targets

(continued from previous page)

I can define common organizational/formatting structures (e.g., headings, graphics, multimedia) and determine the structure(s) that will allow me to organize my complex ideas so that each new element builds on what precedes it. (R)

I can analyze the information, identify domain-specific vocabulary for my topic, incorporate techniques such as metaphor, simile, and analogy, and organize information into broader categories using my chosen structure(s). (R)

I can present my information maintaining an objective tone and formal style that includes an introduction that previews what is to follow, supporting details, varied transitions and syntax (to clarify and create cohesion when I move from one idea to another), and a concluding statement/section that supports the information presented. (P)

W

W.11-12.2 *(cont.)*

© 2011 Align, Assess, Achieve, LLC

Writing

CCR

Write narratives to develop real or imagined experiences or events using effective technique, well-chosen details, and well-structured event sequences.

Standard

Write narratives to develop real or imagined experiences or events using effective technique, well-chosen details, and well-structured event sequences.

a. Engage and orient the reader by setting out a problem, situation, or observation and its significance, establishing one or multiple point(s) of view, and introducing a narrator and/ or characters; create a smooth progression of experiences or events.

b. Use narrative techniques, such as dialogue, pacing, description, reflection, and multiple plot lines, to develop experiences, events, and/or characters.

c. Use a variety of techniques to sequence events so that they build on one another to create a coherent whole and build toward a particular tone and outcome (e.g., a sense of mystery, suspense, growth, or resolution).

d. Use precise words and phrases, telling details, and sensory language to convey a vivid picture of the experiences, events, setting, and/or characters.

e. Provide a conclusion that follows from and reflects on what is experienced, observed, or resolved over the course of the narrative.

*These broad types of writing include many subgenres. See Appendix A for definitions of key writing types.

Enduring Understanding

Writing should be purposely focused, detailed, organized, and sequenced in a way that clearly communicates the ideas to the reader.

Essential Questions

What do good writers do?
What's my purpose and how do I develop it?

Suggested Learning Targets

I can define narrative and describe the basic parts of plot (exposition, rising action, climax, falling action, and resolution). (K)

(continued on next page)

Vocabulary

narrative, point of view, coherent

W

W.11-12.3

© 2011 Align, Assess, Achieve, LLC

Writing

CCR

Write narratives to develop real or imagined experiences or events using effective technique, well-chosen details, and well-structured event sequences.

Standard

Write narratives to develop real or imagined experiences or events using effective technique, well-chosen details, and well-structured event sequences.

a. Engage and orient the reader by setting out a problem, situation, or observation and its significance, establishing one or multiple point(s) of view, and introducing a narrator and/ or characters; create a smooth progression of experiences or events.

b. Use narrative techniques, such as dialogue, pacing, description, reflection, and multiple plot lines, to develop experiences, events, and/or characters.

c. Use a variety of techniques to sequence events so that they build on one another to create a coherent whole and build toward a particular tone and outcome (e.g., a sense of mystery, suspense, growth, or resolution).

d. Use precise words and phrases, telling details, and sensory language to convey a vivid picture of the experiences, events, setting, and/or characters.

e. Provide a conclusion that follows from and reflects on what is experienced, observed, or resolved over the course of the narrative.

*These types of writing include many subgenres. See Appendix A for definitions of key writing types.

Suggested Learning Targets

(continued from previous page)

I can engage the reader by introducing one or more point(s) of view, the narrator (first, second, or third person point of view), characters, setting (set the scene), and a problem, situation, or observation and its significance. (S)

I can use narrative techniques (e.g., dialogue, pacing, description, reflection, and/or multiple plot lines) to develop experiences, events, and/or characters. (S)

I can use descriptive words and phrases that reveal details, appeal to the senses, and help convey a vivid picture of the experiences, events, setting, and/or characters (create mind pictures). (S)

I can sequence events and signal changes in time and place by using transition words, phrases, and clauses to show the relationships among experiences and events. (S)

I can create a coherent whole and build toward a particular tone and outcome using a variety of techniques (e.g., repetition, vivid description, point of view). (P)

I can write a logical conclusion that reflects on the experiences/events and provides a sense of closure (ties up all loose ends and leaves the reader satisfied). (P)

W

© 2011 Align, Assess, Achieve, LLC

Writing

CCR

Produce clear and coherent writing in which the development, organization, and style are appropriate to task, purpose, and audience.

Standard

Produce clear and coherent writing in which the development, organization, and style are appropriate to task, purpose, and audience. (Grade-specific expectations for writing types are defined in standards 1–3 above.)

Enduring Understanding

Producing clear ideas as a writer involves selecting appropriate style and structure for an audience and is strengthened through revision and technology.

Essential Questions

Writing clearly: What makes a difference?
Final product: What does it take?

Suggested Learning Targets

I can identify the writing style (argument, informative/explanatory, or narrative) that best fits my task, purpose, and audience. (K)
I can use organizational/formatting structures (graphic organizers) to develop my writing ideas. (S)
I can compose a clear and logical piece of writing that demonstrates my understanding of a specific writing style. (P)

Vocabulary

writing style, task, purpose, audience

W

W.11-12.4

© 2011 Align, Assess, Achieve, LLC

Writing

CCR

Develop and strengthen writing as needed by planning, revising, editing, rewriting, or trying a new approach.

Standard

Develop and strengthen writing as needed by planning, revising, editing, rewriting, or trying a new approach, focusing on addressing what is most significant for a specific purpose and audience. (Editing for conventions should demonstrate command of Language standards 1–3 up to and including grades 11-12.)

Enduring Understanding

Producing clear ideas as a writer involves selecting appropriate style and structure for an audience and is strengthened through revision and technology.

Essential Questions

Writing clearly: What makes a difference?

Final product: What does it take?

Suggested Learning Targets

- I can use prewriting strategies to formulate ideas (e.g., graphic organizers, brainstorming, lists). (S)
- I can recognize that a well-developed piece of writing requires more than one draft. (K)
- I can apply revision strategies (e.g., reading aloud, checking for misunderstandings, adding and deleting details) with the help of others. (S)
- I can edit my writing by checking for errors in capitalization, punctuation, grammar, spelling, etc. (S)
- I can analyze my writing to determine if my purpose and audience have been fully addressed and revise when necessary. (R)
- I can prepare multiple drafts using revisions and edits to develop and strengthen my writing. (P)
- I can recognize when revising, editing, and rewriting are not enough, and I need to try a new approach. (R)

Vocabulary

revision strategy, edit, purpose, audience

W

W.11-12.5

© 2011 Align, Assess, Achieve, LLC

Writing

CCR

Use technology, including the Internet, to produce and publish writing and to interact and collaborate with others.

Standard

Use technology, including the Internet, to produce, publish, and update individual or shared writing products in response to ongoing feedback, including new arguments or information.

Enduring Understanding

Producing clear ideas as a writer involves selecting appropriate style and structure for an audience and is strengthened through revision and technology.

Essential Questions

Writing clearly: What makes a difference?

Final product: What does it take?

Suggested Learning Targets

I can identify technology (e.g., Word, Publisher, PowerPoint, wiki, blog) that will help me produce, publish, and update my individual or shared writing products. (K)

I can determine the most efficient technology medium to complete my writing task. (R)

I can respond to ongoing feedback and/or new arguments or information to produce, publish, and update my writing projects. (S)

Vocabulary

feedback

W

W.11-12.6

© 2011 Align, Assess, Achieve, LLC

Writing

CCR

Conduct short as well as more sustained research projects based on focused questions, demonstrating understanding of the subject under investigation.

Standard

Conduct short as well as more sustained research projects to answer a question (including a self-generated question) or solve a problem; narrow or broaden the inquiry when appropriate; synthesize multiple sources on the subject, demonstrating understanding of the subject under investigation.

Enduring Understanding

Effective research presents an answer to a question, demonstrates understanding of the inquiry, and properly cites information from multiple sources.

Essential Questions

What do good researchers do?
"Cut and Paste:" What's the problem?

Suggested Learning Targets

I can define research and distinguish how research differs from other types of writing. (K)

I can focus my research around a problem to be solved, a central question that is provided, or a self-generated question I have determined (e.g., *How did Edgar Allan Poe's life experiences influence his writing style?*). (S)

I can choose several sources (e.g., biographies, non-fiction texts, online encyclopedia) and synthesize information to answer my research inquiry. (S)

I can determine if I need to narrow or broaden my inquiry based on the information gathered. (R)

I can create a research paper/project to demonstrate understanding of the subject under investigation. (P)

Vocabulary

research, central question, synthesize

| W | W.11-12.7 |

© 2011 Align, Assess, Achieve, LLC

Writing

CCR

Gather relevant information from multiple print and digital sources, assess the credibility and accuracy of each source, and integrate the information while avoiding plagiarism.

Standard

Gather relevant information from multiple authoritative print and digital sources, using advanced searches effectively; assess the strengths and limitations of each source in terms of the task, purpose, and audience; integrate information into the text selectively to maintain the flow of ideas, avoiding plagiarism and overreliance on any one source and following a standard format for citation.

Enduring Understanding

Effective research presents an answer to a question, demonstrates understanding of the inquiry, and properly cites information from multiple sources.

Essential Questions

What do good researchers do?
"Cut and Paste:" What's the problem?

Suggested Learning Targets

- I can determine the credibility of a source by reviewing who wrote it, when it was written, and why it was written. (R)
- I can assess the strengths and limitations of my sources to determine those that are most appropriate for my task, purpose, and audience avoiding overreliance on any one source. (S)
- I can use advanced searches with multiple authoritative print and/or digital sources effectively to gather information needed to support my research. (S)
- I can define plagiarism (using someone else's words/ideas as my own). (K)
- I can avoid plagiarism by paraphrasing (putting in my own words) and/or summarizing my research findings. (S)
- I can determine when my research data or facts must be quoted (directly stated "word for word") and integrate the information into my text to maintain the flow of ideas. (S)
- I can follow a standard format for citation to create a bibliography for sources that I paraphrased or quoted in my writing. (K)

Vocabulary

credibility, overreliance, advanced search, plagiarism, paraphrase, authoritative print

W

W.11-12.8

© 2011 Align, Assess, Achieve, LLC

Writing

CCR

Draw evidence from literary or informational texts to support analysis, reflection, and research.

Standard

Draw evidence from literary or informational texts to support analysis, reflection, and research.

a.   Apply *grades 11–12 Reading standards* to literature (e.g., "Demonstrate knowledge of eighteenth-, nineteenth- and early-twentieth-century foundational works of American literature, including how two or more texts from the same period treat similar themes or topics").

b.   Apply *grades 11–12 Reading standards* to literary nonfiction (e.g., "Delineate and evaluate the reasoning in seminal U.S. texts, including the application of constitutional principles and use of legal reasoning [e.g., in U.S. Supreme Court Case majority opinions and dissents] and the premises, purposes, and arguments in works of public advocacy [e.g., *The Federalist*, presidential addresses]").

Enduring Understanding

Effective research presents an answer to a question, demonstrates understanding of the inquiry, and properly cites information from multiple sources.

Essential Questions

What do good researchers do?
"Cut and Paste:" What's the problem?

Suggested Learning Targets

I can define textual evidence ("word for word" support). (K)

I can determine textual evidence that supports my analysis, reflection, and/or research. (R)

I can compose written responses and include textual evidence to strengthen my analysis, reflection, and/or research. (P)

Vocabulary

textual evidence, analysis, reflection, research

W   W.11-12.9

© 2011 Align, Assess, Achieve, LLC

Writing

CCR

Write routinely over extended time frames (time for research, reflection, and revision) and shorter time frames (a single sitting or a day or two) for a range of tasks, purposes, and audiences.

Standard

Write routinely over extended time frames (time for research, reflection, and revision) and shorter time frames (a single sitting or a day or two) for a range of tasks, purposes, and audiences.

Enduring Understanding

Effective writers use a variety of formats to communicate ideas appropriate for the audience, task, and time frame.

Essential Questions

Why write?
What do good writers do?

Suggested Learning Targets

I can determine a writing format/style to fit my task, purpose, and/or audience. (R)
I can recognize that different writing tasks (e.g., journal, reflection, research) require varied time frames to complete. (R)
I can write for a variety of reasons (e.g., to inform, to describe, to persuade, to entertain/convey an experience). (P)

Vocabulary

writing format, writing style, task, purpose, audience

W
W.11-12.10
© 2011 Align, Assess, Achieve, LLC

Speaking and Listening

CCR

Prepare for and participate effectively in a range of conversations and collaborations with diverse partners, building on others' ideas and expressing their own clearly and persuasively.

Standard

Initiate and participate effectively in a range of collaborative discussions (one-on-one, in groups, and teacher-led) with diverse partners on *grades 11–12 topics, texts, and issues,* building on others' ideas and expressing their own clearly and persuasively.

a. Come to discussions prepared, having read and researched material under study; explicitly draw on that preparation by referring to evidence from texts and other research on the topic or issue to stimulate a thoughtful, well-reasoned exchange of ideas.

b. Work with peers to promote civil, democratic discussions and decision-making, set clear goals and deadlines, and establish individual roles as needed.

c. Propel conversations by posing and responding to questions that probe reasoning and evidence; ensure a hearing for a full range of positions on a topic or issue; clarify, verify, or challenge ideas and conclusions; and promote divergent and creative perspectives.

d. Respond thoughtfully to diverse perspectives; synthesize comments, claims, and evidence made on all sides of an issue; resolve contradictions when possible; and determine what additional information or research is required to deepen the investigation or complete the task.

Enduring Understanding

Comprehension is enhanced through a collaborative process of sharing and evaluating ideas.

Essential Questions

What makes collaboration meaningful? Making meaning from a variety of sources: What will help?

Suggested Learning Targets

I can review and/or research material(s) to be discussed and determine key points and/or central ideas. (S)

(continued on next page)

Vocabulary

civil, democratic discussion, synthesize

SL

SL.11-12.1

© 2011 Align, Assess, Achieve, LLC

Speaking and Listening

CCR

Prepare for and participate effectively in a range of conversations and collaborations with diverse partners, building on others' ideas and expressing their own clearly and persuasively.

Standard

Initiate and participate effectively in a range of collaborative discussions (one-on-one, in groups, and teacher-led) with diverse partners on grades 11–12 topics, texts, and issues, building on others' ideas and expressing their own clearly and persuasively.

a. Come to discussions prepared, having read and researched material under study; explicitly draw on that preparation by referring to evidence from texts and other research on the topic or issue to stimulate a thoughtful, well-reasoned exchange of ideas.
b. Work with peers to promote civil, democratic discussions and decision-making, set clear goals and deadlines, and establish individual roles as needed.
c. Propel conversations by posing and responding to questions that probe reasoning and evidence; ensure a hearing for a full range of positions on a topic or issue; clarify, verify, or challenge ideas and conclusions; and promote divergent and creative perspectives.
d. Respond thoughtfully to diverse perspectives; synthesize comments, claims, and evidence made on all sides of an issue; resolve contradictions when possible; and determine what additional information or research is required to deepen the investigation or complete the task.

Suggested Learning Targets

(continued from previous page)

I can create questions and locate key textual evidence to contribute to a discussion on the given topic, text, or issue. (P)

I can work with peers to define the rules and roles necessary to promote civil, democratic discussions and decision-making. (S)

I can come prepared with key points and textual evidence to contribute to a discussion and stimulate a thoughtful well-reasoned exchange of ideas. (S)

I can participate in a discussion by posing questions that connect the ideas of several speakers, responding to questions, and elaborating on my own ideas and/or the ideas of others to ensure a full range of positions on a topic or issue. (S)

I can propel conversations by clarifying, verifying, or challenging ideas and conclusions to promote divergent and creative perspectives. (S)

I can respond thoughtfully to diverse perspectives; synthesize comments, claims, and evidence; resolve contradictions when possible; and determine when additional information or research is required. (S)

© 2011 Align, Assess, Achieve, LLC

Speaking and Listening

CCR

Integrate and evaluate information presented in diverse media and formats, including visually, quantitatively, and orally.

Standard

Integrate multiple sources of information presented in diverse formats and media (e.g., visually, quantitatively, orally) in order to make informed decisions and solve problems, evaluating the credibility and accuracy of each source and noting any discrepancies among the data.

Enduring Understanding

Comprehension is enhanced through a collaborative process of sharing and evaluating ideas.

Essential Questions

What makes collaboration meaningful? Making meaning from a variety of sources: What will help?

Suggested Learning Targets

I can identify various purposes (e.g., to inform, to persuade, to describe, to convey an experience) for presenting information to a reader or audience. (K)
I can analyze the information presented in diverse media and formats (e.g., charts, graphs, tables, websites, speeches) and integrate the information in order to make informed decisions and solve problems. (R)
I can evaluate the credibility and accuracy of various presentations and note any discrepancies. (S)

Vocabulary

discrepancy

SL

SL.11-12.2

© 2011 Align, Assess, Achieve, LLC

Speaking and Listening

CCR

Evaluate a speaker's point of view, reasoning, and use of evidence and rhetoric.

Standard

Evaluate a speaker's point of view, reasoning, and use of evidence and rhetoric, assessing the stance, premises, links among ideas, word choice, points of emphasis, and tone used.

Enduring Understanding

Comprehension is enhanced through a collaborative process of sharing and evaluating ideas.

Essential Questions

What makes collaboration meaningful? Making meaning from a variety of sources: What will help?

Suggested Learning Targets

I can define point of view as how the speaker feels about the situation/topic being presented. (K)

I can determine a speaker's point of view (*What do I know about the speaker's opinions, values, and/or beliefs?*) and explain his/her reasoning. (R)

I can define rhetoric (a technique used to persuade a listener to consider a topic from a different perspective). (K)

I can identify when a speaker uses evidence and/or rhetoric and analyze how these techniques strengthen his/her point of view or purpose. (R)

I can assess the stance, premises, links among ideas, word choice, points of emphasis, and tone used by the speaker. (S)

Vocabulary

point of view, rhetoric

SL

SL.11-12.3

© 2011 Align, Assess, Achieve, LLC

Speaking and Listening

CCR

Present information, findings, and supporting evidence such that listeners can follow the line of reasoning and the organization, development, and style are appropriate to task, purpose, and audience.

Standard

Present information, findings, and supporting evidence, conveying a clear and distinct perspective, such that listeners can follow the line of reasoning, alternative or opposing perspectives are addressed, and the organization, development, substance, and style are appropriate to purpose, audience, and a range of formal and informal tasks.

Enduring Understanding	Essential Questions
Presentation of knowledge and ideas is enhanced through appropriate organization and style for an audience via the use of visual displays, technology, and the appropriate use of language.	What makes a presentation "great"? "What I say" versus "how I say it", does it really matter?

Suggested Learning Targets

I can present information, findings, and/or supporting evidence clearly, concisely, and logically to convey a clear and distinct perspective. (S)

I can present my information in a sequence that allows the listener to follow my line of reasoning. (S)

I can address alternative or opposing perspectives in my presentation. (S)

I can prepare a presentation with organization, development, substance, and style that are appropriate to purpose, task, audience, and a range of formal and informal tasks. (P)

Vocabulary

line of reasoning, perspective, task, purpose, audience

SL   SL.11-12.4

© 2011 Align, Assess, Achieve, LLC

Speaking and Listening

CCR

Make strategic use of digital media and visual displays of data to express information and enhance understanding of presentations.

Standard

Make strategic use of digital media (e.g., textual, graphical, audio, visual, and interactive elements) in presentations to enhance understanding of findings, reasoning, and evidence and to add interest.

Enduring Understanding

Presentation of knowledge and ideas is enhanced through appropriate organization and style for an audience via the use of visual displays, technology, and the appropriate use of language.

Essential Questions

What makes a presentation "great"?
"What I say" versus "how I say it", does it really matter?

Suggested Learning Targets

I can identify the parts of my presentation, including findings, reasoning, and evidence, that could use clarification, strengthening, and/or additional interest. (K)
I can integrate appropriate digital media in a strategic manner to improve my presentation. (S)

Vocabulary

digital media

SL

SL.11-12.5

© 2011 Align, Assess, Achieve, LLC

Speaking and Listening

CCR

Adapt speech to a variety of contexts and communicative tasks, demonstrating command of formal English when indicated or appropriate.

Standard

Adapt speech to a variety of contexts and tasks, demonstrating a command of formal English when indicated or appropriate. (See grades 11-12 Language standards 1 and 3 for specific expectations.

Enduring Understanding

Presentation of knowledge and ideas is enhanced through appropriate organization and style for an audience via the use of visual displays, technology, and the appropriate use of language.

Essential Questions

What makes a presentation "great"?
"What I say" versus "how I say it", does it really matter?

Suggested Learning Targets

I can identify various reasons for speaking (e.g., informational, descriptive, formal, informal). (K)
I can determine speaking tasks that will require a formal structure. (R)
I can compose a formal speech that demonstrates a command of grades 11-12 Language standards. (P)

Vocabulary

formal, informal

© 2011 Align, Assess, Achieve, LLC

Language

| Conventions of Standard English

CCR

Demonstrate command of the conventions of standard English grammar and usage when writing or speaking.

Standard

Demonstrate command of the conventions of standard English grammar and usage when writing or speaking.

    a.   Apply the understanding that usage is a matter of convention, can change over time, and is sometimes contested.

    b.   Resolve issues of complex or contested usage, consulting references (e.g., *Merriam-Webster's Dictionary of English Usage, Garner's Modern American Usage*) as needed.

See ELA CCSS Appendix A, page 31 for Language Progressive Skills that require continued attention in grades 11-12.

Enduring Understanding

Effective communication of ideas when speaking or writing relies on the appropriate use of the conventions of language.

Essential Questions

Why do the rules of language matter? Communicating clearly: What does it take?

Suggested Learning Targets

I can recognize that the conventions of standard English usage can change over time (e.g., British users of standard English write *colour*, while American users of standard English have changed the spelling and write *color*.). (R)

I can recognize that certain standard English usage can be contested, and individuals can dispute what is correct/proper (e.g., Many grammarians have argued that we should not split infinitives because split infinitives were not permissible in Latin. However, modern authors often split infinitives because it creates a more rhythmic flow to the writing – *to boldly go where no man has gone before*.). (R)

I can consult reference materials to resolve issues of complex or contested usage of standard English. (S)

Vocabulary

convention, contested

L

L.11-12.1

© 2011 Align, Assess, Achieve, LLC

Language

CCR

Demonstrate command of the conventions of standard English capitalization, punctuation, and spelling when writing.

Standard

Demonstrate command of the conventions of standard English capitalization, punctuation, and spelling when writing.

a. Observe hyphenation conventions.
b. Spell correctly.

Enduring Understanding

Effective communication of ideas when speaking or writing relies on the appropriate use of the conventions of language.

Essential Questions

Why do the rules of language matter? Communicating clearly: What does it take?

Suggested Learning Targets

I can determine when to capitalize words (e.g., proper nouns, "I", first word in a sentence). (K)

I can apply common hyphenation conventions (e.g., dividing a word at the end of a line between syllables, compound numbers from twenty-one to ninety-nine, spelled out fractions, certain compound nouns). (S)

I can recognize that there are many different rules concerning hyphens and use resources to assist me in hyphenating correctly. (R)

I can identify misspelled words and use resources to assist me in spelling correctly. (S)

Vocabulary

hyphen, convention

L

L.11-12.2

© 2011 Align, Assess, Achieve, LLC

Language

CCR

Apply knowledge of language to understand how language functions in different contexts, to make effective choices for meaning or style, and to comprehend more fully when reading or listening.

Standard

Apply knowledge of language to understand how language functions in different contexts, to make effective choices for meaning or style, and to comprehend more fully when reading or listening.

a. Vary syntax for effect, consulting references (e.g., *Tufte's Artful Sentences*) for guidance as needed; apply an understanding of syntax to the study of complex texts when reading.

Enduring Understanding

Effective readers, writers, and listeners use knowledge of language to make appropriate choices when presenting information and to clarify meaning when reading or listening.

Essential Questions

How does situation affect meaning?
How does author's choice impact an audience?

Suggested Learning Targets

I can identify how language functions in different contexts. (K)
I can analyze the context of various texts and determine how language choice affects meaning, style, and comprehension. (R)
I can explain that syntax refers to how words are arranged to form sentences. (K)
I can identify regular/normal syntax (a basic pattern of subject, verb, object). (K)
I can identify irregular/varied syntax (placing words in varying order). (K)
I can write using varied syntax and consult references for guidance as needed. (S)
I can recognize that writers creatively use irregular/varied syntax to convey imagery, to create rhyme scheme, to emphasize ideas, etc. (R)

Vocabulary

syntax

© 2011 Align, Assess, Achieve, LLC

Language

CCR

Determine or clarify the meaning of unknown and multiple-meaning words and phrases by using context clues, analyzing meaningful word parts, and consulting general and specialized reference materials, as appropriate.

Standard

Determine or clarify the meaning of unknown and multiple-meaning words and phrases based on *grades 11–12 reading and content,* choosing flexibly from a range of strategies.

    a. Use context (e.g., the overall meaning of a sentence, paragraph, or text; a word's position or function in a sentence) as a clue to the meaning of a word or phrase.

    b. Identify and correctly use patterns of word changes that indicate different meanings or parts of speech (e.g., *conceive, conception, conceivable*).

    c. Consult general and specialized reference materials (e.g., dictionaries, glossaries, thesauruses), both print and digital, to find the pronunciation of a word or determine or clarify its precise meaning, its part of speech, its etymology, or its standard usage.

    d. Verify the preliminary determination of the meaning of a word or phrase (e.g., by checking the inferred meaning in context or in a dictionary).

Enduring Understanding

Effective readers and writers use knowledge of the structure and context of language to acquire, clarify, and appropriately use vocabulary.

Essential Questions

When a word doesn't make sense, what can I do?
How do I use what I know to figure out what I don't know?

Suggested Learning Targets

I can infer the meaning of unknown words using context clues (e.g., definitions, synonyms/ antonyms, restatements, examples found in surrounding text). (R)

I can recognize and define common affixes and roots (units of meaning). (K)

I can break down unknown words into units of meaning to infer the definition of the unknown word. (S)

I can use patterns of word changes to determine a word's meaning or part of speech. (S)

I can verify my inferred meaning of an unknown word, its part of speech, its etymology, and/ or its standard usage by consulting general and specialized reference materials (e.g., dictionaries, glossaries, thesauruses). (K)

Vocabulary

affix, root, etymology

L

L.11-12.4

© 2011 Align, Assess, Achieve, LLC

Language

CCR

Demonstrate understanding of word relationships and nuances in word meanings.

Standard

Demonstrate understanding of figurative language, word relationships, and nuances in word meanings.

a. Interpret figures of speech (e.g., hyperbole, paradox) in context and analyze their role in the text.
b. Analyze nuances in the meaning of words with similar denotations.

Enduring Understanding

Effective readers and writers use knowledge of the structure and context of language to acquire, clarify, and appropriately use vocabulary.

Essential Questions

When a word doesn't make sense, what can I do?

How do I use what I know to figure out what I don't know?

Suggested Learning Targets

I can define and identify various forms of figurative language (e.g., simile, metaphor, hyperbole, personification, alliteration, onomatopoeia). (K)

I can interpret figures of speech (sometimes what you say is not exactly what you mean) and analyze their overall role in the text. (R)

I can recognize word relationships and use the relationships to further understand multiple words (e.g., *sympathetic/apathetic*). (R)

I can recognize the difference between denotative meanings (all words have a dictionary definition) and connotative meanings (some words carry feeling). (K)

I can analyze how certain words and phrases that have similar denotations (definitions) can carry different nuances (subtle shades of meaning, feeling, or tone). (R)

Vocabulary

figure of speech, word relationships, denotation, nuance

L   L.11-12.5

© 2011 Align, Assess, Achieve, LLC

Language

CCR

Acquire and use accurately a range of general academic and domain-specific words and phrases sufficient for reading, writing, speaking, and listening at the college and career readiness level; demonstrate independence in gathering vocabulary knowledge when encountering an unknown term important to comprehension or expression.

Standard

Acquire and use accurately general academic and domain-specific words and phrases, sufficient for reading, writing, speaking, and listening at the college and career readiness level; demonstrate independence in gathering vocabulary knowledge when considering a word or phrase important to comprehension or expression.

Enduring Understanding

Effective readers and writers use knowledge of the structure and context of language to acquire, clarify, and appropriately use vocabulary.

Essential Questions

When a word doesn't make sense, what can I do?
How do I use what I know to figure out what I don't know?

Suggested Learning Targets

I can recognize the difference between general academic words and phrases (Tier Two words are subtle or precise ways to say relatively simple things, e.g., *saunter* instead of *walk*.) and domain-specific words and phrases (Tier Three words are specific to content knowledge, e.g., *lava, legislature, carburetor*.).* (R)
I can acquire and use college and career readiness level academic and domain-specific words/phrases to demonstrate proficiency in reading, writing, speaking, and listening.
I can consider vocabulary knowledge including denotation, nuance, etymology, etc. and determine the most appropriate words or phrases to express overall meaning. (S)
I can gather vocabulary knowledge independently when considering a word or phrase important to comprehension or expression. (S)

*Tier One, Tier Two, and Tier Three words are clarified on pages 33-35 of Appendix A in the Common Core Standards.

Vocabulary

general academic words, domain-specific words

L   L.11-12.6

© 2011 Align, Assess, Achieve, LLC